SCHOLASTIC

Teaching Reading With Rosemary Wells Books

BY **R**EBECCA **D**E**A**NGELIS **C**ALLAN
AND **L**AURIE **D**E**A**NGELIS

Northern Plains Public Library
Ault Colorado

NEW YORK • TORONTO • LONDON • AUCKLAND • SYDNEY
MEXICO CITY • NEW DELHI • HONG KONG • BUENOS AIRES

Teaching
Resources

For Henry and Jillian
and their super-duper dad

–RDC

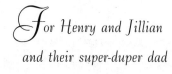 *In Memory of Jean M. Piccioli*
1933–2004

Chris — Let the adventure continue! Here's to the next 20 years!
Julie — What more can I say? ~ Aboosta. You are the best!

–LPD

A SPECIAL THANKS TO ROSEMARY WELLS FOR HER COMMITMENT TO LITERACY.

Cover from NOISY NORA (Original edition) by Rosemary Wells. Copyright © 1973 by Rosemary Wells. Used by permission of Dial Books for Young Readers, a division of Penguin Young Readers Group, a member of Penguin Group (USA) Inc., 345 Hudson Street, NY, NY 10014. All rights reserved.

Cover from NOISY NORA (with all new illustrations) by Rosemary Wells. Copyright © 1973 by Rosemary Wells, text. Copyright © 1997 by Rosemary Wells, illustrations. Used by permission of Dial Books for Young Readers, a division of Penguin Young Readers Group, a member of Penguin Group (USA) Inc., 345 Hudson Street, NY, NY 10014. All rights reserved.

Cover from TIMOTHY GOES TO SCHOOL by Rosemary Wells. Copyright © 1981 by Rosemary Wells. Used by permission of Dial Books for Young Readers, a division of Penguin Young Readers Group, a member of Penguin Group (USA) Inc., 345 Hudson Street, NY, NY 10014. All rights reserved.

Rosemary Wells photo courtesy of Penguin Putnam, © Nelvana Productions. Profile of Rosemary Wells adapted from *The Big Book of Picture-Book Authors & Illustrators*, by James Preller (Scholastic Professional Books, 2001). Reprinted by permission of James Preller.

"Feelings" by Betsy Franco from THEMATIC POETRY: ALL ABOUT ME! Copyright © 2000 by Betsy Franco. Reprinted by permission of the author.

"Money" from 50 LEARNING SONGS SUNG TO FAVORITE TUNES by Meish Goldish. Copyright © 2001 by Meish Goldish. Reprinted by permission of Scholastic Inc.

Edited by Joan Novelli.
Cover and interior design by Kathy Massaro.
Interior art by Maxie Chambliss.

ISBN 13: 978-0-439-59023-5
ISBN 10: 0-439-59023-X

Copyright © 2007 by Rebecca DeAngelis Callan and Laurie DeAngelis.
All rights reserved. Published by Scholastic Inc.
Printed in the U.S.A.

1 2 3 4 5 6 7 8 9 10   40   15 14 13 12 11 10 09 08 07

Contents

A Look Inside This Book

Author-illustrator Rosemary Wells has written and illustrated more than 60 books for children—heartening stories with characters and story lines that invite readers to explore some of the more ticklish themes of childhood: feelings, friendship, and family. This book takes a close look at ten Rosemary Wells favorites, with lessons and reproducible activity pages that support the language arts standards. (See page 5 for connections to the standards.)

The Rosemary Wells books featured in this resource are available at many school and public libraries. And some are likely tucked in your bookshelves, waiting to be rediscovered. Whether you're using Rosemary Wells titles to build an author study or simply to share a beloved read-aloud, this book has ideas and activities you can turn to again and again. You'll find engaging lessons and interactive reproducible activity pages for teaching reading with Rosemary Wells books, as well as many great ideas for connecting literature with math, social studies, science, and other areas of the curriculum. Here's a sampling of what's inside:

- **Meet Rosemary Wells:** Share this interview to help children answer their questions about a favorite author. To learn more, visit the Web sites noted on page 5.

- **Activities to Use With Any Book:** From predicting and sequencing to summarizing and synthesizing, these activities are designed to strengthen essential reading skills.

- **Before Reading:** Use the suggestions for introducing each book to teach essential reading skills, such as predicting, using prior knowledge, and previewing.

- **After Reading:** Use the discussion starters as a guide to take a closer look at text features, picture clues, vocabulary, character development, and more.

- **Extension Activities:** For each featured title, several step-by-step extension activities provide further support for strengthening reading skills and making connections to other areas of the curriculum.

- **Reproducible Activity Pages:** These ready-to-use pages encourage independent learning with activity sheets, manipulatives, templates, and other materials designed to strengthen reading, writing, and more.

- **Author Study Celebration:** Wrap up your study of Rosemary Wells with engaging activities designed to celebrate students' learning (pages 63–64).

Connections to the Language Arts Standards

Mid-continent Research for Education and Learning (McREL), a nationally recognized nonprofit organization, has compiled and evaluated national and state standards—and proposed what teachers should provide for their students to grow proficient in language arts, among other curriculum areas. The activities in this book support these standards for grades K–1 in the following areas:

Reading

- ◆ Uses mental images based on pictures and print to aid in comprehension of text
- ◆ Uses meaning clues to aid comprehension and make predictions about content
- ◆ Uses reading skills and strategies to understand and interpret a variety of literary texts
- ◆ Uses reading skills and strategies to understand a variety of familiar literary passages and texts
- ◆ Knows setting, main characters, main events, sequence, and problems in stories
- ◆ Knows the main ideas or theme of a story
- ◆ Relates stories to personal experiences

Writing

- ◆ Uses strategies to organize written work
- ◆ Uses writing and other methods to describe familiar persons, places, objects, or experiences
- ◆ Writes in a variety of forms or genres
- ◆ Writes for different purposes
- ◆ Uses the stylistic and rhetorical aspects of writing
- ◆ Uses descriptive words to convey basic ideas
- ◆ Uses the general skills and strategies of the reading process

Source: *Content Knowledge: A Compendium of Standards and Benchmarks for K–12 Education* (4th ed.). Mid-continent Research for Education and Learning, 2004. For more information about McREL and to learn more about the topics and benchmarks within each language arts standard, visit the Web site at www.mcrel.org.

Learn More About Rosemary Wells

Children's Literature
(www.childrenslit.com/f_rosemarywells.html)

This Web site, devoted to helping readers make knowledgeable choices about children's literature, offers critical reviews by authors, librarians, teachers, and other advocates of quality children's literature. The site provides reviews of 33 of Rosemary Wells's books.

Reading Rockets: Launching Young Readers
(www.pbs.org/launchingreaders/rootsofreading/readtogether.html)

You can read an engaging interview with Rosemary Wells at this PBS Web site and view a video clip of the author in her studio, sharing insights into her work as an author and illustrator.

Rosemary Wells: An Artist's Life
(teachingbooks.com/slideshows/wells/Drawing.html)

This link, courtesy of TeachingBooks.net, offers an engaging autobiographical slide show narrated by Rosemary Wells.

The World of Rosemary Wells
(www.rosemarywells.com)

The author's Web site features photographs, biographical information, news about recent releases, games, printable bunny money, and more.

In this book, you'll find several Web site suggestions to support various activities. Please keep in mind that Internet locations and content can change over time. Always check Web sites in advance to make certain the intended information is still available.

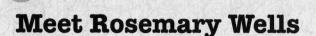

Meet Rosemary Wells

Born: January 29, 1943, in New York, New York
Home: Greenwich, Connecticut

Though Rosemary Wells is both a writer and an illustrator, she firmly believes that the story is the central part of a good picture book. "The misconception is that it is relatively easy to write for children, that illustrating is the hard part. I believe the opposite is true," she states. "The words come first. The story begins with feelings and is embellished with humor, adventure, and character. The words it takes to bring these elements to life are paramount. When they are truly well done, the book becomes poetry."

According to Rosemary, writing for children is much more difficult than writing for adults. The main reason: A children's book must remain enjoyable even after it has been read aloud 500 times!

To create her stories, Rosemary often draws upon episodes in her own life and the lives of her two daughters, Victoria and Meg. A family pet and his heirs also play important roles. Rosemary explains, "Our West Highland white terrier, Angus, had the shape and expressions to become Benjamin, Tulip, and Timothy, and all the other animals I have made up for my stories. He also appears as himself in a couple of books."

Although Rosemary will sometimes get an idea from observing her own children, she believes that "it's much more important to have been a child than to have children. It's because I was a child and I'm very close to that time in my life that I can do this. Incidents from childhood are universal."

While she stresses that each book has a logic of its own—"there is no single way of doing it"—Rosemary usually begins by focusing on one particular character. "The central issue in all my books is emotional content," she says. "I continually pick similar themes. One of the themes I use a lot is belonging to a group or feeling that you don't belong."

Like most writers, Rosemary takes small incidents—a snatch of overheard conversation, a long-held memory, an amusing thought—and runs them through to their logical conclusions in her mind. "When my daughter Beezoo (Meg) was in second grade, she wanted more than anything to take in her favorite stuffed animal for show-and-tell. She decided against it at the last minute, however, because as she put it, 'The boys would rip it up.'" With that insight in mind, Rosemary wrote *Hazel's Amazing Mother*. "The thing that fiction writers do, of course, is change everything," Rosemary confesses. "We don't write things up as case histories. You change it, reduce it, or embellish it to make the story better."

"Three-quarters of all writing is revising," Rosemary believes. "It's tremendously important to work hard, to practice, and to revise—to do things again and again and again until they are right. You can't just snap it out and say it's going to be right the first time. It isn't right," she says, matter-of-factly, "until it's right."

"When I go to workshops for young writers, I bring a kaleidoscope with a detachable end, but I don't tell them it's a kaleidoscope at first," Rosemary explains. "Then I show them a handful of junk—paper clips, little plastic files, a couple of buttons—the kind of stuff you might find at the bottom of a drawer and throw out. I tell them that when you put all these different shapes and colors into the kaleidoscope, and you hold it up to your eyes, you make a rose window." Rosemary pauses a moment to make her point: "Everybody makes a different window," she says. "You turn the kaleidoscope and the exact image can never be repeated again. The design is yours to make from the ordinary essence of life. That's what writing is about."

Rosemary Wells photo courtesy of Penguin Putnam, © Nelvana Productions. Profile of Rosemary Wells adapted from *The Big Book of Picture-Book Authors & Illustrators*, by James Preller (Scholastic Professional Books, 2001). Reprinted by permission of James Preller.

Activities to Use With Any Book

Each of Rosemary Wells's more than 60 books offers exciting opportunities to enliven lessons in the classroom. The suggestions below may be used with any Rosemary Wells book to learn more from the story.

Teaching With the Pictures

Strengthen a range of skills with a look at a book's illustrations, beginning with the cover.

◎ **Predicting:** Examine the book's cover. Before reading the book, invite students to name titles of other books they've read by Rosemary Wells. Ask: "What do you notice about the cover of this book? What does this picture suggest this book might be about? What does Rosemary Wells want us to know before we begin reading?"

◎ **Observing:** Take a picture walk. Before reading the book, encourage students to share observations about what is happening in the pictures. Ask: "What information is the author sharing with us in this illustration?"

◎ **Problem Solving:** Use illustrations as support for reading text. Illustrations frequently provide students with insights into the meaning of words they read. After reading the book aloud, discuss ways in which the words are supported by the illustrations. Students may find this strategy helpful, especially when they encounter unfamiliar words.

Exploring the Story

From predicting and sequencing to summarizing and synthesizing, here are some ways to use the books to build strong reading skills.

◎ **Predicting:** What might happen next? Encourage students to think about what has happened in the story so far. Ask: "Where in the text or illustrations can we find clues about what might happen?" Then ask: "Why does your prediction make sense?" Use the What's Ahead? reproducible (page 10) to help children develop thoughtful predictions.

◎ **Sequencing:** Invite students to fill in the What Happened When? graphic organizer (page 10) to recall a story's sequence of events—from what happened in the beginning to what happened at the end. Or explore plot sequence with Pocket Chart Retellings (page 9).

◎ **Organizing Data:** Have students create a story map to record what they know about story elements, including characters, plot, setting, and theme. For an extra challenge, invite children to provide specific details from the story.

◎ **Retelling:** Retelling a story's plot not only deepens a reader's comprehension but also offers an opportunity for you to assess a child's understanding. Take the retelling process a step further by having students put their retellings into writing.

◎ **Conflict and Resolution:** Will Ruby have what she needs to make Grandma a birthday cake? Will Timothy make a friend at school? Having characters encounter problems is a familiar plot device—and with each turn of the book's pages suspense grows. Have students identify the most important problem in a story and offer alternate solutions.

◎ **Synthesizing:** Use A Rosemary Wells Review (page 11) to encourage children to reflect on and respond to the stories they read.

Mind's Eye Scenes (Language Arts, Art)

Use visual representation to assess children's comprehension.

1. Provide students with paper, pencils, and crayons or markers. Explain that while you read a story aloud, children will be drawing.

2. To help children prepare their papers for the drawing activity, demonstrate how to draw two lines (through the center) to divide their paper into four squares. Have children write the title of the book at the top of the page and then number each square 1 through 4.

3. Explain that as you read the book aloud, you'll stop reading four times. Each time you'll ask students to draw a picture that depicts the events from the story in one of the numbered boxes. (Rather than showcasing Rosemary Wells's illustrations, encourage children to draw their own visualizations.)

4. Read a few pages of the story and stop. Ask students to create a picture to show what happened. To check comprehension, you may want to ask volunteers to describe their drawings. Or observe what individual children draw and invite them to point out details and explain the illustration. For example, after reading the first few pages of *Timothy Goes to School*, a student may draw Timothy sitting alone. A thought bubble above Timothy's head may depict a sad Claude, sitting alone at an enormous lunch table.

5. When all four drawings are complete, have children write (or dictate) a sentence to describe what is happening in the scene. As you assess student work, consider whether each child demonstrates understanding of the story's characters, setting, and events.

Pocket Chart Retellings (Language Arts)

Strengthen understanding of story structure and summarizing skills with this activity.

1. As a group, summarize the story's beginning, middle, and end. Record each sentence on a sentence strip.

2. Let students retell the story by placing the sentence strips in order in a pocket chart. Use this activity to reinforce time order words—what happened first, second, next, and so on. For early readers, you may want to invite students to illustrate key words from the story. For example, if you're working on retelling *Yoko*, have a child draw a picture of a lunchbox beside each occurrence of the word *lunch*.

3. As you reread the book aloud, encourage children to keep an eye on the pocket chart. Invite volunteers to point out important events in the story. Record those events on sentence strips, and invite volunteers to make adjustments to the sentence order.

4. Further strengthen sequencing and oral language skills by inviting children to revisit the pocket chart with partners to arrange the sentence strips in order. (Mix them up first.)

Character Queries (Language Arts)

Play an engaging guessing game that invites children to think about book characters and ask (and answer) questions.

1. In advance, prepare five 3- by 18-inch strips of oak tag to use as headbands. Explain to the group that you will be playing a guessing game in which students reflect on information about characters in a Rosemary Wells book they just read. Have children identify the characters in the story. Record the name of each character on a separate headband.

2. To start, choose one student to put on a headband (without peeking at the name of the character that's printed on it). The child wearing the headband asks yes or no questions about the character, such as "Do I go to Hilltop School?" or "Am I the best at everything I do?" The other children respond to the student's questions.

3. When the child who is guessing has identified the character listed on his or her headband, it's time for another student to take a turn. Continue playing as time allows or until all the characters in the story have been guessed. For a greater challenge, write the names of characters on the headbands in advance, without student input. Or use this activity with characters from several books.

Name _____ Date _____

What's Ahead?

Write the book's title: _____

Explain what happened in the story so far: _____

_____

_____

On the back of this page:

1. Draw a picture of what you think will happen next.

2. Write a sentence that describes what is happening in your picture.

✂ --

Name _____ Date _____

What Happened When?

Write the book's title: _____

Explain what happened in the beginning. _____

_____

Explain what happened next. _____

_____

Explain what happened at the end. _____

_____

On the back of this page: Draw a picture to show what happened at the end.

Name _____ Date _____

A Rosemary Wells Review

What did you think about the book you just read? Write a book review by answering these questions.

1 Which Rosemary Wells book did you read?

Title: _____

2 Who was your favorite character?

Name: _____

3 On the back of this page draw a picture of this character. Include details that tell something about this character.

4 Why did you like this character? Explain.

_____

_____

5 Who would enjoy reading this book? Why?

_____

_____

6 What else should readers know about this book?

_____

_____

Teaching Reading With Rosemary Wells Books © 2007 by Rebecca DeAngelis Callan and Laurie DeAngelis, Scholastic Teaching Resources

Timothy Goes to School

◆◆◆

(PENGUIN PUTNAM, 1981)

Messages and Themes

- Often friendships form when least expected.

- Other people may share your frustrations with a particular situation or problem.

Additional Rosemary Wells books that feature Timothy are:

Adding It Up
(Viking, 2001)

Discover and Explore
(Viking, 2oo1)

How Many? How Much?
(Puffin & Viking, 2001)

Letters and Sounds
(Viking, 2001)

Ready to Read
(Viking, 2001)

Timothy's Tales From Hilltop School
(Viking, 2002)

World Around Us
(Viking, 2001)

When Timothy's teacher makes the prediction that Timothy and Claude will be "the best of friends," she's mistaken. Claude meets Timothy's eagerness for a new friend with criticism and indifference. Timothy is disappointed again and again . . . until he makes a friend of his own, Violet.

Before Reading

As a group, discuss the first day of school—meeting new people, eating lunch, having circle time, and playing at recess. Show children the cover of the book. Then invite students to notice each character's facial expression, share how that character might be feeling, and make predictions about what will happen to those characters in the story.

After Reading

Help children compare their predictions about the story to what actually took place between Timothy and Claude, and Timothy and Violet. To encourage students to make important connections between the story and their own lives, examine Rosemary Wells's illustrations of Timothy's school. Invite children to find common features. To help children continue to make connections, use the following discussion starters:

◎ What are some of the ways that Timothy tries to fit in at school?

◎ Discuss how Claude treats Timothy. Ask: Have you ever known someone like Claude or Grace? How did you feel around him or her? Why?

◎ Invite children to describe both friendly and unfriendly behavior. Use this as an opportunity to discuss strategies for dealing with bullying.

Feelings Pictograph (Math)

As a group, create a pictograph. Use the graph to show and compare Timothy's feelings before and after his first four days at Hilltop School.

1. In advance, draw a face on each of eight index cards (four happy and four sad). Show the cards to students and explain that children will be using these cards to keep track of Timothy's feelings.

2. Revisit the picture book. Invite volunteers to explain how Timothy felt before and after each day, pointing out evidence from the story (illustrations or text) to support their opinions. Have each volunteer select a card that shows Timothy's mood, and then place the card on the graph, beside the appropriate school day. For example, in a discussion about Timothy's feelings before the first day of school, a volunteer looking at the illustrations may point out that Timothy is smiling. This volunteer would select a card that reflects Timothy's feelings (a happy face card) and tape it to the pictograph.

3. Continue in this manner until all eight cards are on the pictograph. Invite students to discuss the graph, tally the total number of happy faces and sad faces. Ask: "What did you discover?"

How Did Timothy Feel About School?

	Before School	After School
Day 1	:)	:(
Day 2	:)	:(
Day 3	:)	:(
Day 4	:(	:)

Matching Words and Feelings

(Language Arts)

Children match faces to feelings with this vocabulary-building activity.

1. Gather the following materials: five paper dessert plates and five blank sentence strips. On each of the paper plates, draw a face that illustrates a particular feeling (happy, sad, angry, and so on). On each of the sentence strips, write the word that names each feeling pictured.

2. As a group, discuss different kinds of feelings and ways of using facial expressions and body language to recognize feelings.

mad
happy

(continued)

3. Display the pictures and words. Invite children to act out each of the five feelings pictured.

4. In random order, place the plates and sentence strips in a pocket chart. Have children match each face with the corresponding word.

5. For an extra challenge, place plates, sentence strips, and writing supplies in a basket near the pocket chart. Encourage students to create additional feelings plates and sentence strips to rearrange and match.

Guess How I Feel? (Social Studies)

Help children learn how to read body language and facial expressions with a game of pretend.

1. Write names for different feelings on index cards (one per card). You may want to choose feelings that are straightforward for students to emote. For example, a student who draws an "angry" card may have an easier time pretending to be angry than a child who draws a "frustrated" card.

2. Place the index cards in a bowl, and have a volunteer choose one. Have this child use facial expressions and body language to dramatize the feeling on the card. When ready, the performing student asks the rest of the group to guess how he or she feels.

3. The child who guesses the performer's feeling correctly takes the next turn.

First-Rate-Friend Flyers (Language Arts, Social Studies)

Timothy's first few days of school didn't go well until he met Violet . . . and made a friend. Explore qualities that make someone a good friend.

1. Ask students to think about what made Violet a good friend for Timothy. Then as a class, brainstorm qualities that describe a true friend.

2. Give each child a copy of the flyer template (page 16).

3. Have students use the page to write an advertisement or flyer that shows what makes them special as a friend. Encourage students to use descriptive words such as *honest, brave,* and *funny* instead of vague words such as *nice* and *good.*

4. When the flyers are complete, display them in the classroom for children to enjoy and read.

Feelings and Favorite Shirts

(Language Arts, Art)

Help students better understand what they read with an activity that encourages them to make connections to characters in the story.

1. As a group, retell Timothy's third day of school. (Timothy wears his favorite shirt—a white shirt with blue stripes.)

2. Give each child a copy of the shirt template (page 17), along with crayons or markers. Explain that children will be drawing a picture of a favorite shirt and then completing two descriptive sentences. In their writing, encourage students to include key details. To explain why the shirt is a favorite, for example, a child may write " . . . because my grandmother Abby brought me the shirt all the way from Australia." To complete the second sentence, a child may write: "When I wear my favorite shirt, I feel strong and brave."

3. When students are ready, invite them to share their work. To help children draw even more connections between their own lives and the life of the character Timothy, invite them to wear a favorite shirt to school the next day. Take a photograph if possible, and display it alongside a copy of the book in the classroom library.

Book Links

Chrysanthemum
by Kevin Henkes
(William Morrow, 1996)

Being teased about her name is no fun for a mouse named Chrysanthemum. When at last the dejected mouse meets her music teacher, Mrs. Delphinium Twinkle, everything changes for the better.

The Kissing Hand
by Audrey Penn
(Child Welfare League of America, 1995)

A mother raccoon reassures her son and helps him overcome his anxieties about going to school.

A First-Rate Friend

Draw a picture of yourself in the frame. Then write answers to the questions below.

1 My name is _____ .

2 My favorite thing to do is _____ .

3 I am an expert at _____

_____ .

4 I'm a good friend because _____

_____ .

5 Three words that describe me are:

_____   _____   _____

Three words that do not describe me are:

_____   _____   _____

Teaching Reading With Rosemary Wells Books © 2007 by Rebecca DeAngelis Callan and Laurie DeAngelis, Scholastic Teaching Resources

Name _____ Date _____

My Favorite Shirt

Draw a picture of your favorite shirt. Then use lots of details to complete the sentences below.

This shirt is my favorite because

_____

_____

_____ .

When I wear this shirt, I feel _____

_____

_____

_____ .

Emily's First 100 Days of School

(HYPERION, 2000)

Messages and Themes

◆ People encounter numbers in every setting.

◆ People use numbers to count, estimate, measure, and more.

Every day is one day closer to the hundredth day of school, a day Emily's class will celebrate with a big party.

Before Reading

Show children the book's cover. Invite volunteers to point out key details in the illustration, such as the rabbit seated at a desk and the numerals printed along the border. Let students share predictions about the story's setting, characters, and subject. Then show students the numerals on the book's end pages and title page. Invite students to make new or revised predictions about the book.

After Reading

As a group, compare predictions about the book with what occurred in the story. Revisit the book's cover, end pages, and title page. Discuss the ways in which some book features may offer a reader clues about a story's setting, characters, and subject matter. Use the following questions to continue to discuss the book and make connections:

◎ If you were Emily, what would you have brought to Miss Cribbage's classroom? Why?

◎ Have you celebrated One Hundred Days before? What kinds of things did you do to learn about the number 100?

◎ Where in Emily's classroom do you see numbers? Where in our classroom do you see numbers?

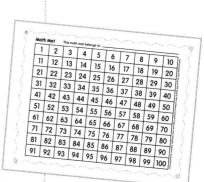

Ten Sets of Ten Critters (Language Arts, Math)

Invite students to put their math skills into action and show what they know about animals and creepy crawlies by making this mini-book. Predictable text on each page assists young readers.

1. Have children brainstorm different kinds of critters. Record responses on chart paper. Post the chart where children can readily refer to it.

2. Give each child a copy of the mini-book text boxes (page 21) and 12 sheets of paper. (Depending on how much room students need to write, use half or full pages.) Have students cut out the text boxes and glue one to the top of each sheet of paper, then place the pages in order and staple to bind.

3. Have students complete the cover by writing their name and filling in the date. Then read aloud each question. As a group, discuss and solve the first question. Display a measure of ten centimeters for reference. Have volunteers name ten critters that are shorter than ten centimeters—for example, caterpillars, ladybugs, salamanders, butterflies, snails, mealworms, houseflies, gnats, hummingbirds, and spiders.

4. Explain how the class's list of critters can help students complete the remaining pages. (You may wish to have students work with a partner to complete their books.) Encourage students to list each kind of critter only once, and to number their sets (1–10) to assist in providing the correct number of responses on each page. When students are finished problem solving and filling in their critter sets pages, discuss the results.

Photo Journals (Math, Language Arts)

Use a digital camera to make a collaborative math journal—and help students learn that numbers are all around them. As a class, take a walk and photograph places where you see numbers in your school (clocks, classroom doors, lockers). Print out the photos, and have children help label each picture. Gather the photographs into a journal, and place the journal in the class library or math center for students to read on their own.

Snack-Time Math Mats (Math)

Help children build math skills with a math mat that doubles as a placemat. Check for food allergies before getting started with this activity.

1. Provide each student with a math mat (page 22). Invite children to make observations about the page. Students may notice, for example, that the grid is set up in ten rows of ten, that all together there are 100 boxes, and that the numerals are in numerical order.

(continued)

Book Links

From One to One Hundred
by Teri Sloat
(Penguin Putnam, 1991)

Imaginative, inventive illustrations elevate this counting book from engaging to irresistible.

100th Day Worries
by Margery Cuyler
(Simon & Schuster, 2000)

For Jessica, finding just the right 100 items for her first-grade class's 100th day celebration is, well, worrisome.

2. To prepare the mats for snack time, have each child personalize his or her mat using crayons or markers. Then laminate the math mats for durability and to create an easy-to-clean surface.

3. When it's time to eat, provide snacks that are easy for small, clean fingers to manipulate, such as dried cherries, cranberries, or blueberries; carob chips; raisins; round- or square-shaped cereal; pieces of popcorn; corn nuts; banana chips; fish-shaped crackers; and pretzels. Have students work with their snacks and mats to practice a variety of math skills. For example, they can estimate ("How many rows do you think your snack will fill up?"), count ("How many pretzels do you have? How many will be left if you eat five?"), and arrange sets of ten ("How many sets of ten raisins are there? How many are left over?").

On the Way to One Hundred Day

As a class, you may enjoy any or all of these activities while on your way to One Hundred Day.

◎ Have children bring in collections of 100 nonfood items, such as postcards, stickers, and seashells. Provide children with an opportunity to share their collections with classmates.

◎ Gather 100 signatures on a greeting card for your school principal or the town mayor. Invite the special recipient to visit the classroom after the card arrives.

◎ Ask students to collect, count, and sort 100 items, such as keys, buttons, or bread bag tags.

◎ Encourage children to practice estimating distance. Mark the length of the playground or hallway. Then use a trundle wheel to take the actual measurement. (Check to see if the school has one you can borrow.) Consider having the child whose estimate is closest to the actual measurement place a sign at the 100-foot mark.

◎ Invite students to use 100 items in a structure—items such as blocks to create a castle, cubes to build a tower, and links to build a paper chain.

◎ Write a long list on chart paper. As a group, brainstorm a list of 100 things—books to read, people to meet, places to visit, games to play, and so on. (You may need a few sheets of chart paper for this activity!)

①

Ten Sets of Ten Critters

Name _____

Date _____

②

Ten critters that are shorter than 10 centimeters:

③

Ten critters that are longer than 10 centimeters:

④

Ten critters that are longer than my foot:

⑤

Ten critters that weigh less than an apple:

⑥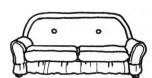

Ten critters that weigh more than a sofa:

⑦

Ten critters that take up more space than a beach ball:

⑧

Ten critters that take up less space than a soup can:

⑨

Ten critters that move faster than a rabbit:

⑩

Ten critters that move slower than a squirrel:

⑪

Ten critters that live within one mile of my home:

⑫ Count the critters' names on pages 2–11. Then fill in the blank.

All together I've thought of

_____ critters!

Math Mat

This math mat belongs to: _____

1	2	3	4	5	6	7	8	9	10
11	12	13	14	15	16	17	18	19	20
21	22	23	24	25	26	27	28	29	30
31	32	33	34	35	36	37	38	39	40
41	42	43	44	45	46	47	48	49	50
51	52	53	54	55	56	57	58	59	60
61	62	63	64	65	66	67	68	69	70
71	72	73	74	75	76	77	78	79	80
81	82	83	84	85	86	87	88	89	90
91	92	93	94	95	96	97	98	99	100

Noisy Nora

◆◆

(PENGUIN PUTNAM, 1973)

N ora had to wait . . . and wait . . . and wait for the attention she craved from her parents, who were trying to meet the needs of Nora's siblings.

Messages and Themes

◆ Sometimes the way a person behaves gives us clues about how he or she feels.

◆ There are appropriate ways to let people know you need their help or attention.

Before Reading

Invite volunteers to tell about a time when they felt left out. Encourage students to explain what they did about it, if anything. Share the book cover and read the title, and then ask children what they think is happening. Remind students to think about their ideas as you read, to see if their predictions are correct.

After Reading

Use these questions to guide a discussion about some of the choices Nora made in the story (being disruptive to gain attention from her family, leaving the house for a few minutes, returning home).

◎ How does Nora feel at the beginning of the story? At the end? How do you know?

◎ What else could Nora have done besides making noise while she waited and waited?

◎ How do you feel when you have to wait for a long time?

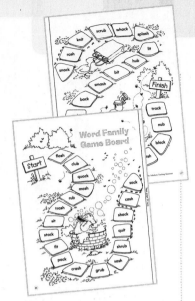

Tip

▲▲▲▲▲▲

A phonogram is a letter or series of letters that stands for a sound or series of sounds. For example, the letters -ay in say stand for the long-a sound. The letters -ack in pack stand for two sounds: /a/ and /k/. Words with the same phonogram or rime (such as pack, stack, and back) belong to the same word family. The word rime can be used in place of phonogram. In a syllable, the rime is the vowel and everything after it. In the word pack, the rime is -ack. (The letter p is referred to as the onset.)

Rime Cube

Word Family Board Game (Language Arts)

Help students put their rhyming know-how into action with this engaging board game for two to four players. Note: This game board is designed to reinforce phonograms in *Noisy Nora*. To adapt the game to reinforce other phonograms, simply use liquid eraser to replace the words on the game board and the rimes on the game cube.

1. Photocopy and color the game board (pages 26–27). Glue the game board patterns together where indicated, and laminate for durability. To make the rime cube, copy the pattern (below) and glue it to oak tag. Cut out the pattern along the solid lines. Fold along the dotted lines to form a cube, and then secure the edges with tape. Prepare a game board and rime cube for each group of two to four players.

2. To introduce the game, reread *Noisy Nora*. Draw students' attention to words that sound alike. Point out that some of those words are spelled differently and others share the same rime or word family ending. Explain that as they play the Word Family Board Game, students will learn about words with the same ending. (To give children practice with identifying a word family, you may have them brainstorm words that share the rime -ick, such as *wick*, *chick*, and *pick*.)

3. To play, have each child choose a game marker (such as a penny or counter) and place it on the spot marked Start. Players take turns rolling the cube and reading the rime on the top of the cube. The player advances his or her marker to the first square on the board that contains a word with a matching rime (-ack, -it, -ub, or -ash).

4. The game continues in this way until all players reach the final space on the game board (*track*).

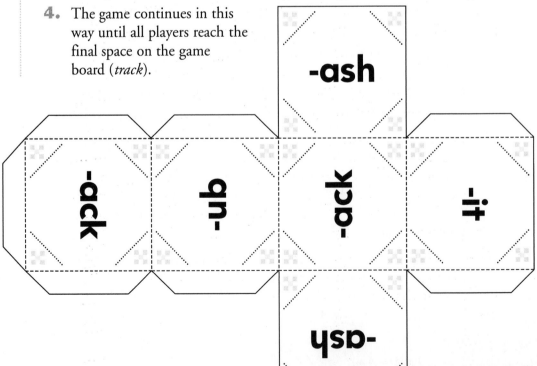

Some Quiet Advice (Language Arts)

Ask students to imagine that they have a friend who behaves the same way as Nora, making lots and lots of noise. Explain that sometimes friends, especially friends like Noisy Nora, need encouraging advice. Tell children that each of them will be writing a letter of advice to Nora, offering his or her sensible opinions about the nature of Nora's problem and what to do about her impatience—instead of being noisy.

1. As a group, talk about the letter's format and content. Then, on a sheet of chart paper, create a template with students: Discuss and record where to write the date, greeting, salutation, and signature.

2. Next, talk about what kind of information each paragraph should include. In the first paragraph, you may have children describe the problem (in their own opinion) to Nora. In the second paragraph, you may have students offer Nora a few alternatives to being disruptive.

3. Give each child a copy of the letter pattern (page 62; mask the title and the picture postage stamps at the top of the page before photocopying). Explain to students that they can use the pattern as stationery for writing their own letters to Nora. Show children how to fold the letter pattern in thirds, write an address on the front, and compose a letter on the inside.

Just-Like-Nora Narratives (Language Arts)

Students use *Noisy Nora* as inspiration for their own stories about a personal memory.

1. Encourage children to think about the main character in the story, Nora. Ask: "How does Nora feel about waiting . . . and waiting? How do Nora's actions in the story show us how she feels? What do you suppose Nora is waiting for?"

2. Invite students to write about a time they felt just like Nora and what they did about it. One child, for example, may write about a time he or she was extremely frustrated while standing in the checkout line at the grocery store for what seemed like an eternity. Another might write about how hard it is to wait for a parent to get off the phone.

3. As they write, encourage students to think about where they were (setting), what happened (events), and how their actions help show readers how they feel.

Book Links

Clarice Bean: That's Me
by Lauren Child
(Candlewick, 1999)

It isn't easy for Clarice to locate some peace and quiet in a home chock-full of familial hullabaloo.

Lilly's Purple Plastic Purse
by Kevin Henkes
(Greenwillow, 1996)

Lilly finds she simply cannot wait for sharing time to show off her new purse—and makes a few decisions she soon regrets.

Word Family Game Board

Start

flash

club

quack

mash

rub

trash

sit

stack

fit

pack

crash

grub

sash

shrub

quit

shack

cash

sack

Tape page 27 here.

26

scrub

whack

knit

splash

rash

lit

snack

hub

bit

smash

Finish

back

stub

track

tack

nub

cub

black

split

tub

dash

Yoko

◆◆

(HYPERION, 1998)

Messages and Themes

◆ People enjoy eating different kinds of food.

◆ An unfamiliar food may be a tasty treat.

▲▲▲▲▲▲▲▲▲▲▲

Additional Rosemary Wells books that include the character Yoko are:

Yoko and Friends School Days: Doris's Dinosaur
(Hyperion, 2001)

Yoko and Friends School Days: The Germ Busters
(Hyperion, 2002)

Yoko and Friends School Days: The Halloween Parade
(Hyperion, 2001)

Yoko and Friends School Days: Mama, Don't Go!
(Hyperion, 2001)

Yoko and Friends School Days: The School Play
(Hyperion, 2001)

Yoko's Paper Cranes
(Hyperion, 2001)

▼▼▼▼▼▼▼▼▼▼▼

Yoko is excited about her day at Hilltop School until lunchtime, when the other children begin teasing her about the foods inside her willow-covered cooler.

Before Reading

Talk with students about the title and cover of the book. Have them predict what this book is about. Have they heard the name Yoko before? What is the character holding in her hand? What do they suppose is inside the cooler?

After Reading

Invite students to examine the illustrations and notice the ways in which Yoko shows her feelings (happiness, sadness, disappointment) in the story. Encourage children to make connections between the events in the story and the way Yoko's feelings change over time. Use the following prompts to go further:

◎ What would you do if your classmates teased you about your favorite foods? How would you feel?

◎ When Mrs. Jenkins held International Food Day in the classroom, she thought she'd solved Yoko's problem, but she hadn't quite. Have you ever tried to solve a problem, only to discover it hasn't been solved at all? Describe what happened.

◎ Describe a time you tasted an unfamiliar food. What surprised you about this food?

Chez Kids (Social Studies, Language Arts)

Transform the dramatic play area of your classroom into a restaurant that reinforces reading and writing skills.

1. Have students gather and arrange props (cookware, hats, pretend food) to create a restaurant in the classroom. If children feel that key tools and equipment of a real-life restaurant are absent, invite them to improvise with classroom materials and supplies. For example, if young waiters wish they had menus, provide them with large sheets of oak tag. To make menus, children can draw pictures or cut out pictures from magazines of foods they want to include, then organize them on the oak tag by categories before gluing them in place. If they wish, children can label the foods, add mouthwatering descriptions, and list prices.

2. Stir up students' appetites for exploring the new center by taking a class field trip to a local restaurant. Or take a tour of the school's cafeteria. When you return to the classroom, encourage children to discuss the experience— what they were surprised to learn and their favorite parts of the adventure. Then provide students with opportunities for playing and learning in their classroom's dining establishment.

3. Use the restaurant as a source of ongoing active learning experiences. Children can write and read orders, follow directions to cook up the specials, write (and read) the daily specials on a small whiteboard, and read recipe books.

Multicultural Recipes (Language Arts, Social Studies)

As a class, make a collaborative cookbook to help children share some of the favorite recipes their families enjoy.

1. Give each student a large index card to take home. Ask children to work with family members to record the name of the dish, information about serving size, ingredients, and step-by-step directions on how to make it. Work with children who are unable to bring in a family recipe to create a card for a favorite dish.

2. Place all the recipe cards in a recipe box. (A square storage container works well.) Label the box with a title, such as "Our Favorite Recipes."

3. To build reading skills, place the box in a center and invite students to sort the recipes in a variety of ways. For example, you may have children place the recipes in alphabetical order or sort recipes by the type of food (dessert, meat dish, bread, and so on). To build science and math skills, you may have students select a recipe and then help you prepare the favorite food as a snack. To wrap up this activity, make photocopies of the class cookbook to share with families.

Favorite Foods Interviews (Language Arts)

Help children develop interviewing skills as they discover how many food favorites they have in common.

1. Give each student a copy of the interview form (page 32).

2. Explain that children will interview each other to find out what foods they enjoy. Tell students to dig for details as they interview their partners and fill in the answers on the interview form. For example, a child responding to an interview question about a favorite dessert may volunteer "ice cream" as an answer. The interviewer's role is to find out specifics—for example, by asking "What flavor of ice cream is your favorite?" or "What is your favorite way to enjoy ice cream?"

3. Once the interviewing process is complete, discuss the activity with the group. Encourage students to talk about what it was like to interview a classmate, probe for details, and discuss favorite foods.

Minding Mealtime Manners (Language Arts, Social Studies)

Timothy, who was still hungry, tasted one of Yoko's crab-cones . . . and liked it. But what if he hadn't liked it? What if Timothy had made a sour face and complained loudly to Yoko that he thought all sushi tasted terrible? As a group, discuss what it means to have manners during a meal—what good manners look and sound like. Accept all appropriate student responses, and record them on a sheet of chart paper. Then use the chart as inspiration for some role-playing.

1. Set up a table and chairs at the front of the classroom. Provide mealtime props, such as lunch trays, lunch boxes, cups, and napkins.

2. Choose a scenario to share with students—for example, a student's lunch box contains a meat dish with a strong aroma or a strange-looking fruit, or a classmate has a chocolaty dessert with bright, edible decorations. Invite several children to take a seat at the table and then act out what they would do to be polite in that mealtime situation. Discuss ways in which the role-players used good manners, and then repeat with a new scenario and set of students. As you explore these scenarios as a class, encourage students to be sensitive to cultural differences.

Specific-Feelings Words (Language Arts)

Invite children to look at how Rosemary Wells illustrated Timothy throughout the book. We as readers can see that Timothy's facial expressions and body language show a wide variety of feelings—from looking overjoyed on the first day of school to looking miserable at the end of the second day. Explore words for feelings further with a poem that reminds students of the many ways they can feel!

Feelings

There's happy, embarrassed,
and silly and sad.
There's excited, delighted,
and frightened and glad.

I've had lots of feelings
already today.
And mom says it's only been
half of a day!

by Betsy Franco

Book Links

Abuela
by Arthur Dorros
(Dutton, 1991)

A girl, a grandmother, and an imagination take flight in a memorable story that explores ethnic heritage.

Cloudy With a Chance of Meatballs
by Judi Barrett
(Atheneum, 1978)

What reader could resist an adventure to the town of Chewandswallow, where it rains soup and snows mashed potatoes?

1. In this poem about feelings, the poet uses words like *embarrassed, silly,* and *delighted* to name feelings. Share the poem with students, and invite them to brainstorm other words that describe specific feelings.

2. Make a list of children's word suggestions, and display the list in a writing center.

3. Encourage young poets to use the list as a reference and inspiration for their writing.

Name _____ Date _____

Food Favorites

Interview a classmate about his or her favorite foods. Write each answer below.

I interviewed _____ .

◎ What is your favorite food for breakfast?

_____

◎ What is your favorite food for lunch?

_____

◎ What is your favorite food for dinner?

_____

◎ What is your favorite dessert?

_____

◎ What is your favorite fruit?

_____

◎ What is your favorite vegetable?

_____

◎ What food do you think everyone should try?

_____

Teaching Reading With Rosemary Wells Books © 2007 by Rebecca DeAngelis Callan and Laurie DeAngelis, Scholastic Teaching Resources

McDuff Comes Home

(HYPERION, 1997)

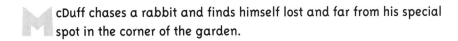 cDuff chases a rabbit and finds himself lost and far from his special spot in the corner of the garden.

Before Reading

Discuss the title of the book with students. Invite children to think about what it means to come home from a faraway place. Where might McDuff go in the story and why? What about the title *McDuff Comes Home* makes you want to read the book?

After Reading

Revisit the title of the book. Encourage students to discuss whether the title fits the story. What else could Rosemary Wells have titled this book? Use the following prompts to further explore the story and help students make connections to the characters.

◎ How do you think McDuff feels when he first sees the rabbit? How do you think he feels when he sees Mrs. Higgins? When he rides on her motorcycle?

◎ There are many books with characters who are curious and many books with characters who get lost. What story or character does *McDuff Comes Home* remind you of? Explain.

◎ In what ways is a person you know similar to Mrs. Higgins? Would you like Mrs. Higgins for a neighbor? Why or why not?

Messages and Themes

◆ It is important to know the address where you live.

◆ People and animals use their senses to gather information.

Additional Rosemary Wells books that include the character McDuff are:

McDuff and the Baby
(Hyperion, 1997)

McDuff Goes to School
(Hyperion, 2001)

McDuff Moves In
(Hyperion, 1997)

McDuff Saves the Day
(Hyperion, 2002)

McDuff's New Friend
(Hyperion, 1998)

The McDuff Stories
(Hyperion, 2000)

Just Like Woof (Language Arts)

Help children use what they already know about onomatopoeia (words that imitate the sounds they name) to think about animals and the noises they make.

1. Provide each child with a copy of Did You Hear That? (page 36). Ask students to imagine that they are listening to the animals in the pictured scene. What sounds would children hear? Students may say words such as *moo, woof,* and *meow.*

2. Encourage children to think about the letters that make those sounds and, in turn, help put together the words. Then have students write noise words in each speech bubble.

3. Use your discussion about sounds as a springboard for discussing noise words in the book *McDuff Comes Home.* You may start the discussion by examining the first page of the book and pointing out the word *zoom.* Before you write the word on chart paper, have students tell what letter sounds they hear in the word.

4. Ask children to suggest other expressive words that remind them of *zoom* (*whoosh, zip, kaboom*). Accept and record students' onomatopoeic words, whether the words are inspired by the McDuff story or are from the story itself.

5. Have children make a word wall by copying the words onto sentence strips, arranging them on a wall space, and adding a title such as "Noise Words."

A Smelling Center (Language Arts, Science)

Use the story as inspiration for creating a smelling center in the classroom that also reinforces content vocabulary.

1. As a group, talk about the five senses (seeing, hearing, smelling, touching, and tasting), and discuss how characters in the book use their senses. Which senses did McDuff, the rabbit, and Mrs. Higgins use? For example, McDuff used his eyes to see a rabbit and his ears to listen to voices inside the house. Explain that you'll be setting up a center in the classroom that invites children to use their sense of smell to do a little sleuthing of their own (like McDuff).

2. Set up a smelling center in your classroom. To start, collect several small, empty opaque containers (such as film canisters) and fill with aromatic, nontoxic items, such as cinnamon sticks, aniseed, onion skins, rosemary stalks, mustard seed, and rose petals. Once the containers are filled, use a nail to poke tiny holes in each lid. Use white glue to secure each lid to the top of its container. Label each container with a letter and make a key for later reference.

3. When the center is ready, invite students to use their sense of smell to try to identify the fragrance in each container. After center time, invite volunteers to share their findings and consult the key to confirm their matches.

An Easy-as-Pie Chart

(Language Arts, Math)

Help students learn that there are lots of ways to organize information into charts and graphs, such as with a pie chart, and reinforce key math vocabulary.

Dog	Cat	Bird	Fish	Other
llll ll	llll	l	llll	lll

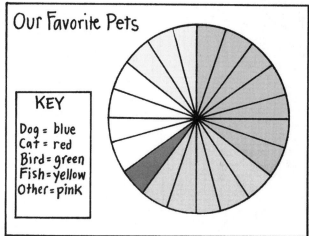

Our Favorite Pets

KEY

Dog = blue
Cat = red
Bird = green
Fish = yellow
Other = pink

1. In advance, prepare a pie chart. Divide the pie chart into as many equal sections as there are students.

2. Tell the class that they will each be voting for their favorite type of pet. Explain that they will be using the results of the vote to make a pie chart.

3. To begin, have each student vote. You may ask, "Raise your hand if your favorite pet is a dog (cat, bird, fish, or other animal)." (Remind children to vote only once.) Tally the votes on chart paper or a whiteboard.

4. Discuss the voting results with the class. Explain that on the pie chart each animal will be represented by a different color, which will make it easy to understand the data they collected. As a group, assign each animal a color—for example, all votes for dogs will be recorded in blue—and create a key for the pie chart.

5. To complete the pie chart, invite a volunteer to identify the total number of votes for one animal and color in that many sections on the pie chart. For example, if seven children voted for a dog as their favorite pet, the volunteer would color seven segments blue. Repeat for each type of pet. Label the chart with a title, such as "Our Favorite Pets."

6. As a group, examine and discuss the pie chart. Invite students to make observations that compare quantities (more than, fewer than, most, least, and so on).

Book Links

Boomer's Big Day
by Constance W. McGeorge
(Raincoast, 1994)

Much to this golden retriever's dismay, his family is moving and his casual lifestyle is turned upside down.

Harry the Dirty Dog
by Gene Zion
(HarperCollins, 1956)

Harry doesn't like to take a bath—that is, until his family doesn't recognize him through his sooty fur.

Did You Hear That?

Think about letter sounds. In each speech bubble, write a word that sounds like the noise that animal makes.

Teaching Reading With Rosemary Wells Books © 2007 by Rebecca DeAngelis Callan and Laurie DeAngelis, Scholastic Teaching Resources

Books Based on the Characters Max and Ruby

Rosemary Wells's most popular books for young children are rooted in the amusing antics of a brother and sister pair of bunnies, Max and Ruby. Use the suggestions below and on pages 38–39 with any Max and Ruby book to support your reading program and build skills across the curriculum. In addition, individual lessons are provided for the following specific Max and Ruby titles:

Read to Your Bunny (page 41)   *Bunny Cakes* (page 53)

Bunny Money (page 45)   *Bunny Mail* (page 59)

Max's Dragon Shirt (page 49)

Bunny Patterns

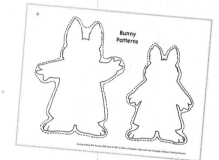

Make several copies of the bunny patterns (page 40) and cut them out. Use the bunny shapes for a variety of instructional purposes. Here are some ideas to get you started:

- **Pocket Chart Pictures:** As a class, summarize the Max and Ruby story you've just read and record the summary on sentence strips. Then, each time one of the bunny's names appears on a sentence strip, place a cutout of the bunny pattern on top of the word. Invite students to read the pocket chart using the rebus picture clues.

- **Favorite Stories Pictograph:** Create a class pictograph of favorite Max and Ruby stories. On chart paper, make a grid with a row for each Max and Ruby book the class has read. Write the title of each book in the first box of each row. Then have each student vote for a favorite book by writing his or her name on a bunny and taping (or gluing) it to the graph. Examine and discuss the results.

- **Bunny-Shaped Mini-Books:** Make mini-books of new Max and Ruby adventures. Provide each child with several copies of the same bunny pattern. Have students align the shapes, staple the bunnies together along the left margin, and then write and illustrate an original story in the booklet.

- **Story Element Strings:** String story elements together for a lively display. Provide each child with pencils, crayons, scissors, tape, four 6-inch lengths of yarn, and a copy (or two) of the bunny patterns. Have students cut out the bunny shapes and

(continued)

then write about a different story element on each bunny (characters, setting, problem, solution). Have children tape a length of yarn to the first bunny shape and then use the second length of yarn to connect that bunny to the second bunny. Clip students' story element strings to a length of clothesline in the classroom.

◎ **Stick Puppet Props:** Invite students to make stick puppets that represent characters from favorite Max and Ruby stories (such as Max, Ruby, Grandma, and the mail carrier), and use them to perform dramatic retellings. For each set of four puppets, you'll need scissors, glue, four craft sticks (tongue depressor–sized), two sheets of construction paper, and copies of the bunny patterns. Guide children in following these steps:

1. Cut out a bunny pattern.

2. Dot glue along half of the craft stick, front and back. Leave the remaining half free of glue.

3. Place the section of the craft stick with glue between the bunny pattern and a half sheet of construction paper. Press it in place.

4. When the glue is dry, trim the construction paper to the puppet's shape. Repeat to make more puppets.

5. Color the puppets with markers, embellish them with yarn, and add other decorative details.

Character Close-Ups (Language Arts, Art)

Invite students to put their investigative skills into action by examining the character traits of Max, Ruby, and Grandma.

1. Give each child a copy of one of the bunny patterns. Explain that to get started on this project, each student will choose one character on which to focus.

2. Provide children with paper, scissors, glue sticks, cotton balls, and other art supplies. (Origami paper and wrapping paper are a fun addition for this activity.) Invite students to refer to illustrations in the Max and Ruby books as they "dress" and add details to the characters they've selected.

3. Give each child a sheet of paper. Have children fold the paper in half and then open it back up (to divide it into halves) or draw a vertical line through the center to divide the page into two sections. Ask students to write their character's name on the left side of the paper and glue their character below. On the right side, have children list a character trait and then provide evidence from two Max and Ruby books.

What-You-Know Webs (Language Arts)

Help students build scaffolding for comprehension with a web-style graphic organizer.

1. Before you read a Max and Ruby story aloud, examine the book's cover with children. Talk about what the subject of the book may be, based on the story's title.

2. Invite students to share what they already know about the subject, and record that information on a web. For example, if you plan to read *Bunny Cakes*, you may write the topic "cakes" in an oval at the center. As students describe what they know about cakes, add that information to the web. For example, a child may suggest that people purchase cakes at a bakery. To record that information, draw a line like the spoke of a wheel, extending from the word *cake*. At the end of it, write "bakery shop." Continue soliciting ideas from students and recording their ideas on the web until the web contains several spokes.

3. As a group, discuss the contents of the web and how the ideas relate to each other. Then read the book, in this case *Bunny Cakes*, aloud.

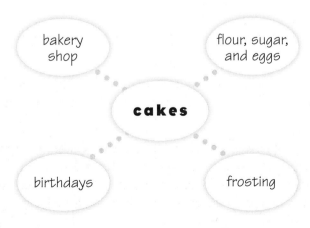

Additional Rosemary Wells books that include the characters Max and Ruby:

Bunny Party (Viking, 2001)

Max and Ruby's Midas (Dial, 1995)

Max Cleans Up (Viking, 2000)

Max Drives Away (Viking, 2003)

Max's Bath (Dial, 1985)

Max's Bedtime (Dial, 1985)

Max's Birthday (Dial, 1985)

Max's Breakfast (Dial, 1985)

Max's Chocolate Chicken (Dial, 1989)

Max's Christmas (Dial, 1986)

Max's Dragon Shirt (Dial, 1991)

Max's First Word (Dial, 1979)

Max's New Suit (Dial, 1979)

Max's Ride (Dial, 1979)

Max's Toys (Dial, 1998)

Ruby's Beauty Shop (Viking, 2002)

Ruby's Tea for Two (Viking, 2003)

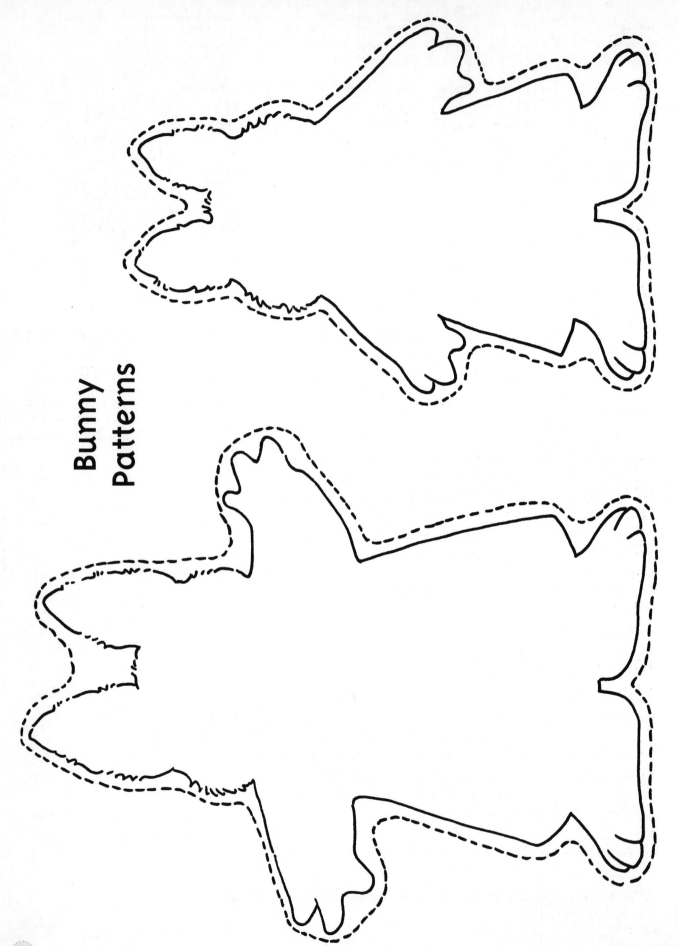

**Bunny
Patterns**

Read to Your Bunny

(SCHOLASTIC, 1998)

This simple, rhyming story shares a message that helped set in motion a national literacy campaign urging families to dedicate 20 minutes a day to reading with children.

Before Reading

When sharing *Read to Your Bunny* or any read-aloud book, try to make the classroom setting more special. Gather students around you. Use desk lamps instead of overhead lighting. Give children ample time to observe and take pleasure in each illustration.

Show students the cover illustration, an adult bunny reading to a child bunny. Invite children to share experiences with reading—who reads them stories, where they read, and the kinds of books they enjoy. While you read the book aloud, invite students to notice all the places the bunnies listen to stories.

After Reading

Invite volunteers to identify all the places where the bunnies enjoyed listening to a story. In a list format, record student responses on chart paper. Review the list with students, and then ask them to think of even more places where it would be fun to read a book. Perhaps they think it would be fun to sit and read in a tree house, a quiet corner, or a cuddly armchair. Add new ideas to the list. Then use these discussion starters to continue to explore what makes reading special:

◎ What are a few of your favorite books? Why are these books special to you?

◎ What do people read besides books? Where else do people find and read printed words?

Messages and Themes

◆ Reading is important.

◆ It's enjoyable to have a special place and time in which to read every day.

Lending Class Books (Language Arts)

Promote reading by creating a lending-library system for the collaborative class books that children make over the course of the school year. You'll need book pockets (one for each book and one for each student), glue sticks, 3- by 5-inch index cards (one for each book), and a large sheet of posterboard. Follow these steps to set up the library:

1. Glue a book pocket to the inside back cover of each book. Write the book's title on an index card and tuck the card inside the pocket.

2. Label the top of the posterboard with a title such as "Our Class Book Library." Have students write their name on a book pocket. Arrange and glue the pockets on the posterboard. (You may organize the pockets into two or three columns.) Place the chart near the classroom library or the area where you keep your class books.

3. Show children how the system works. As a group, look at one of the class books as an example. Point out the inside back cover— how the pocket is attached and how the index card with the title is stored inside the pocket. Explain that each time a child wants to borrow a book, he or she takes the card out of the book's pocket and places it in his or her pocket on the posterboard.

4. To return books, students place the index card back in the book and return it to the class library area.

Bunny Bookmarks (Language Arts)

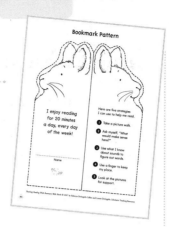

Make bookmarks that help students remember strategies for reading success, and encourage them to read for 20 minutes every day.

1. In advance of making the bookmarks, discuss some techniques students find useful when reading alone or with a family member.

2. Give each child a copy of the bookmark pattern (page 44). Invite children to color the rabbit pictures, sign the back, and then cut out the bookmark pattern along the dotted lines.

3. Have children fold the bookmark along the fold line, turn it facedown on a flat surface, apply glue to each half, and then press the halves together.

4. When the bookmarks are complete, read aloud the five tips with students. Invite volunteers to explain how using each strategy can help them. Definitions from volunteers may be along these lines:

- Taking a picture walk means a reader explores the book page by page, examining the illustrations for clues to the story.

- You can ask yourself, "What would make sense here?" if you get stuck on a word or phrase. Answering the question helps you problem solve and understand what you're reading.

- Pay attention to what you already know about letter sounds, and use that to make sense of words.

- Using a finger to keep your place in the text is giving yourself a pointer, a way of holding your spot while you read.

- Looking at the pictures for support is examining the illustrations for clues. Pictures can help make understanding the text easier.

Tip

▲▲▲▲▲▲

Find out more about Rosemary Wells's national literacy campaign, in which the author advocates families reading together for at least 20 minutes a day. For a further challenge, join Rosemary Wells's efforts and kick off your own version of the reading campaign in your classroom. Begin by sending each student home with his or her bunny bookmark and a note about the importance of spending 20 minutes a day reading. Let families know that they can learn more about the campaign by listening to the author herself at http://teachingbooks.com/slide shows/wells/ReadtoBunny.html.

Book Links

Bedtime for Frances
by Russell Hoban
(Harper, 1960)

A young badger, anxious about noises in the night, puts off her bedtime as long as possible.

A Bedtime Story
by Mem Fox
(Mondo, 1996)

Polly and Bed Rabbit are ready to hear a bedtime story, but are Polly's parents ready?

Bookmark Pattern

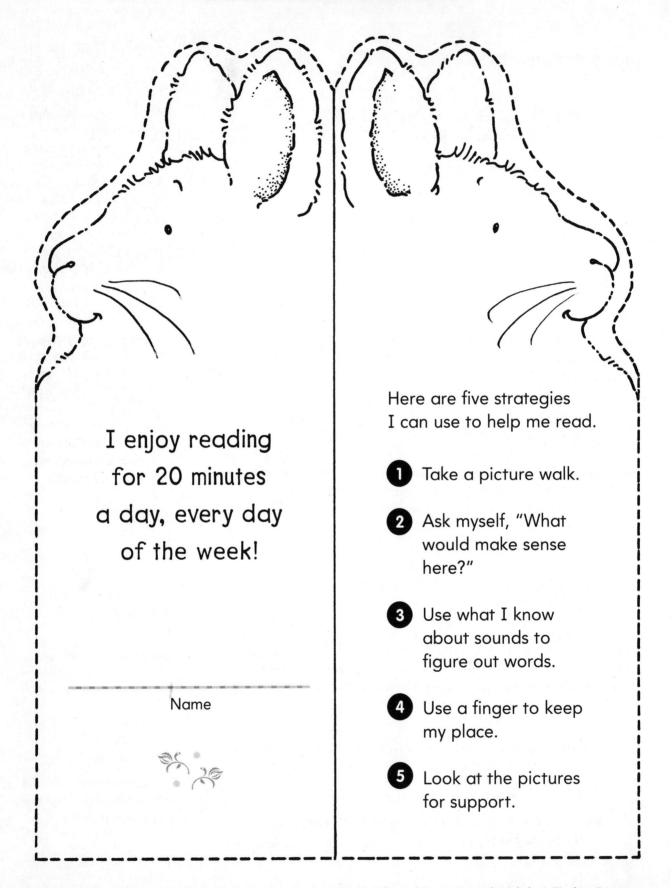

I enjoy reading
for 20 minutes
a day, every day
of the week!

_____
Name

Here are five strategies
I can use to help me read.

1 Take a picture walk.

2 Ask myself, "What
would make sense
here?"

3 Use what I know
about sounds to
figure out words.

4 Use a finger to keep
my place.

5 Look at the pictures
for support.

Bunny Money

(DIAL, 1997)

Ruby's wallet is full of money for Grandma's birthday present. But before long, Max and Ruby are down to a quarter, Max's lucky quarter.

Before Reading

As a group, discuss the experience of shopping for someone else's birthday present. How do you keep from spending too much? Spending too little? Encourage a few volunteers to share their experiences.

After Reading

Discuss the way the author used rebus picture clues to help tell the story. In what ways were the rebus pictures helpful? Confusing? Invite volunteers to show how they used the pictures to help them understand or read the story. Then use the following questions to further explore the story:

◎ How do you know a gift is just right for a person? How do you think Grandma feels about each of the gifts she received from Max and Ruby?

◎ What can readers learn about Grandma by looking at the picture on the last page?

Messages and Themes

· ·

◆ People use money to purchase goods and services.

◆ The value of bills and coins is measured in dollars and cents.

Loose Change (Math)

Provide money (real or play) to explore the theme of the story.

1. Share a variety of real or plastic coins. As a group, discuss each coin's name and monetary value.

2. Place all the coins in a large bowl and mix them up. Tell children that you need their help to sort the coins. Give each student a handful of coins to sort into groups by value or physical attributes (color, size, surface details, or other features).

3. Once children have sorted the coins, invite volunteers to explain how they grouped their coins.

Bunny Banks (Art, Math)

Create Max- and Ruby-shaped piggy banks to reinforce math concepts related to money.

1. Ask families to send in clean plastic containers with lids. (Plastic mayonnaise jars work well for this activity.) To prepare the containers for students, use sharp scissors or a box cutter to make a two-inch hole on the side of the container, a hole long and wide enough for students to fit quarters through easily.

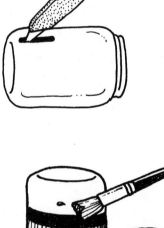

2. Give each child a container. Explain that children will be making bunny banks in which they can save real money. Use an extra container to model steps that follow so that children can follow along.

3. Have children turn their containers upside down. Point out that the lid will be where the bunny's feet are; the bottom of the container will be the bunny's head. The lid (at the bottom) will also provide access to saved coins and bills.

4. Have each child paint his or her bank with tempera or acrylic paints, leaving the lid of the container unpainted. (You might suggest that children remove the lids while painting their containers.) When the banks are dry, have students replace the lids and then glue on playful details to create a Max or Ruby look-alike, such as googly eyes, felt or construction paper ears, cotton ball tails, and pipe cleaner whiskers. Invite children to bring their bunny banks home and begin saving their pocket change!

Bunny Money Manipulatives (Math)

Reinforce key math skills with paper coins that children can work with at their desks or at home.

1. Give each child a copy of the coin patterns (page 48), scissors, tape, and crayons.

2. Have students color their coins and then cut them out along the dashed lines. To make two-sided coins, have children fold the patterns along the solid line and then tape the open sides together.

3. Invite children to practice sorting coins by attribute, adding coin values, and so on.

A Melodic Mnemonic (Language Arts, Math)

Use the power of song to help students retain information about coin values.

1. Give each child a copy of Meish Goldish's song "Money" (below).

2. Explain that students can sing the song to the familiar tune of "Miss Lucy Had a Baby." As a group, hum one verse of "Miss Lucy Had a Baby" to reacquaint children with the tune.

3. Introduce the words to "Money" as a call-and-response activity—with you singing each line and students repeating it aloud. When the group is ready, give singing the whole song a whirl.

Money
(sung to "Miss Lucy Had a Baby")

Miss Lucy had a **penny**,
That means she had a cent.
She kept on saving pennies,
Then to the bank she went.

She traded in her pennies,
And got a **nickel** back.
She kept on saving nickels,
And piled them in a stack.

She traded in her nickels,
And she got back a **dime**.
She saved her dimes and nickels
For a **quarter** over time.

She kept on saving quarters,
And watched her pile increase,
Then traded in her quarters
For a **half-dollar** piece.

Miss Lucy kept on saving,
She saved some more until
She traded her half-dollars
For a single **dollar** bill!

Miss Lucy learned a lesson,
A lesson good to know:
If you save up your money,
Then it will surely grow!

—*Meish Goldish*

Tip

▲▲▲▲▲

Create bunny bills from the end pages of *Bunny Money*. (On the Making Money! page, the author grants children permission to photocopy the end pages of the book and provides easy, step-by-step directions for making one- and five-dollar bunny bills.) If you prefer, visit the author's Web site at rosemarywells.com and click on "Fun With Max and Ruby." There you'll find reproducible templates of Max and Ruby bunny bills and easy how-to directions for making and embellishing the bunny currency.

Book Links

Benny's Pennies
by Pat Brisson
(Doubleday, 1993)

Five shiny new pennies and five modest gifts add up to a memorable story about giving.

26 Letters and 99 Cents
by Tana Hoban
(Greenwillow, 1987)

This engaging book provides a veritable visual feast for readers ready to learn about letters and money.

Bunny Money Manipulatives

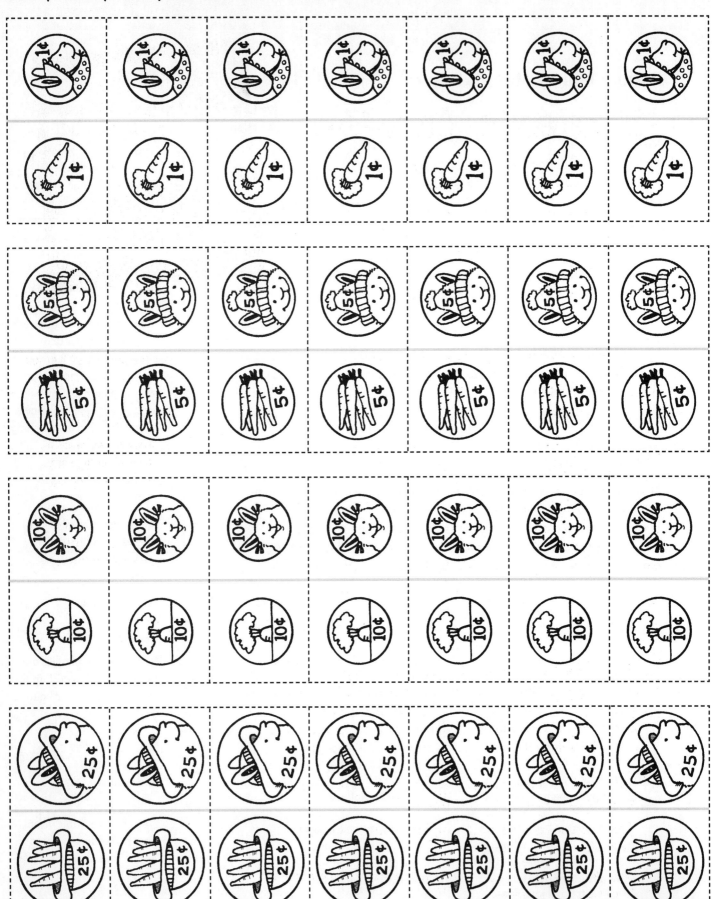

Max's Dragon Shirt

(PENGUIN, 1997)

While on a shopping trip to buy a pair of pants, Max finds himself lost in the Girls' Better Dresses department and becomes the proud owner of a brand-new shirt.

Before Reading

If students have read other books with the character Max, ask them to describe what they know about the character and make predictions about the story's plot. If the class hasn't read other books that feature Max, ask children to make predictions about the story—examining the book's cover and title as a starting point.

After Reading

On the endpapers of the book, there is an illustration of a busy department store. Show students the picture and invite them to make observations about the scene—how the scene may seem familiar, what different groups of rabbits are doing, and so on. Then use the following questions to further discuss the story:

◎ Did Max want a new pair of blue pants? How can we tell how Max felt by looking at the pictures?

◎ If you were Max, what would you have done to find Ruby in the store?

◎ Have you ever been lost in a department store? What did you do to solve the problem?

Messages and Themes

◆ People may purchase clothing at stores.

◆ Every person needs to know his or her name, address, and phone number.

◆ If lost, ask a family member or familiar person older than you to help.

Adjective Word Wall (Language Arts)

Invite students to search the story's text for adjectives—words that describe.

1. Revisit the first page of the story with children and read it aloud. Point out the descriptive words in the text (*old, blue, disgusting*), and record them on chart paper to begin building an adjective word wall based on the book.

2. Turn to the second page of the story and reread the text. Invite students to identify the descriptive words (*brand-new* and *dragon*). Support students' adjective search with directive questions, such as "How does Ruby describe the pants she wants to buy Max?" or "Max wants a specific shirt. What word does he use to describe it?"

3. Continue reading each page of the story, guiding students with questions and recording adjectives on the list. While children may not notice every adjective within the text, they will build awareness that words function in different ways. Display the word wall in a writing center for children's reference. Invite students to use the adjectives in their own writing.

Home-Sweet-Home Mobiles (Health and Safety, Language Arts)

Celebrate safety by making mobiles that help children learn important contact information (name, street address, and phone number). Every student needs to know key details about where he or she lives, especially for emergency situations.

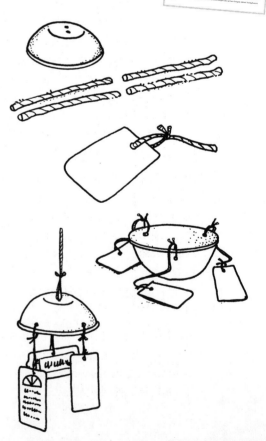

1. Give each student a copy of the mobile patterns (page 52), an eight-inch paper bowl, and a four-foot length of yarn. In advance, punch two holes near the center of each bowl.

2. Have students complete the information on each of the three patterns. Have children cut the yarn into four pieces of approximately the same length and then tape or tie a length of yarn to each shape.

3. Tell children to punch three evenly spaced holes along the bowl's rim. Have children tie the shapes to the bowl.

4. Have students thread the remaining length of yarn through the holes in the bottom of the bowl and tie a knot. Display the mobiles from the classroom ceiling or a length of clothesline. Later, send them home with students to share with families.

Squish-Your-Own Dragon T-Shirts (Art)

Let children make their own dragon shirts. In advance, invite families to send in solid-color T-shirts, googly eyes, and small bottles of fabric paint and fabric glue. (White cotton undershirts work well for this activity.)

1. Have students put on smocks and cover their desks with newspaper.

2. Divide the class into small groups. Provide each group with a few bottles of fabric paint and one T-shirt per child.

3. Tell students that they will be creating dragon face T-shirts in much the same way as they may have made inkblot paintings in the past. To prepare, have students lay their T-shirt flat so that the shirt is faceup and the collar is at the top.

4. Tell children to use a finger to draw a line from the center of the collar down the front of the shirt. (That is where they will be folding shirt, once the paint is applied.) Then have them draw an imaginary circle (about the size of their hand) in the center of the shirt.

5. Invite children to squirt or daub different colors of fabric paint inside the imaginary circle along the fold line. Then have them fold and press the shirt along the fold line, from the collar down to the bottom hem. (Have students press firmly so that the paint colors blend and spread.)

6. Have children carefully open their shirts, keeping the wet, painted sides from touching each other. Use clothespins to hang the shirts on a clothesline. Allow shirts to dry overnight. Children can use fabric glue to attach googly eyes to complete their dragon faces.

7. Send finished shirts home with students. Encourage children to dress like Max from time to time, wearing blue pants and their dragon shirts to school. You may even want to designate one day a month to be a special dragon shirt day.

Book Links

Angus Lost
by Marjorie Flack
(Doubleday, 1932)

Angus, an inquisitive Scottish terrier, explores the world beyond his yard.

The Big Green Pocketbook
by Candice F. Ransom
(HarperTrophy, 1995)

While on a trip to town with her mom, a little girl gathers keepsakes for her very own pocketbook.

Mobile Patterns

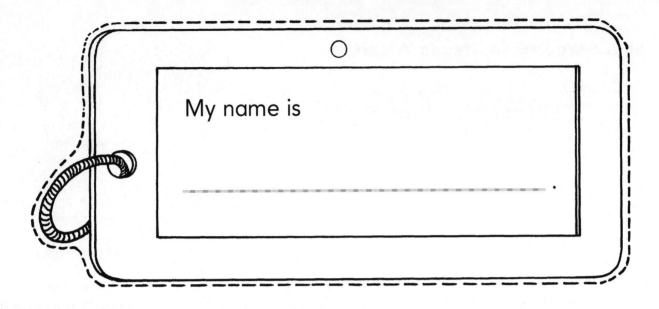

My name is

_____

My phone number is

_____

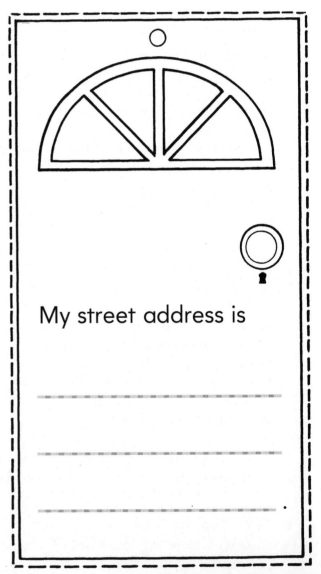

My street address is

_____

_____

_____

Bunny Cakes

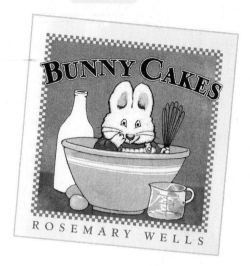

(PENGUIN, 1997)

When Max's "help" in the kitchen becomes too much for Ruby, she sends him to the grocery store with a shopping list of cake ingredients. Some creative problem solving and a lot of determination help Max add one more important ingredient to the list.

Before Reading

Invite children to examine the cover of the book and share observations. They may notice a rabbit (Max), a milk bottle, a whisk, a measuring cup, two brown eggs, and a mixing bowl. Ask students to predict what will happen in the story. If children are familiar with Max, remind them to take his character traits into account as they develop their predictions.

After Reading

As a group, discuss the process of baking a cake (assembling ingredients, gathering measuring tools and ingredients, reading recipes, following directions, and so on). Encourage students to talk about how Ruby prepared to bake her cake for Grandma and how Max tried to "help." Then use the following discussion starters to encourage children to make more connections to the book:

◎ How do you think Max felt when he saw a sign telling him he was not allowed back in the kitchen with Ruby? How would you have felt if you weren't allowed in your family's kitchen?

◎ Most people enjoy eating birthday cake. Would you like to eat Ruby's angel surprise cake with raspberry fluff icing? What about Max's earthworm cake? Explain.

Messages and Themes

◆ When at first people don't understand you, try a different method of telling them what you need. In time, they may understand.

◆ People make mistakes. Sometimes they can make up for their mistakes.

Custom Cake Mix Boxes
(Language Arts, Art)

Have students design their own cake mix boxes, complete with a picture of what the finished cake will look like and an ingredients list.

1. In advance, ask families to send in large empty food boxes. (Cereal, pasta, and granola bar boxes work well.)

2. To introduce the activity, discuss how Max and Ruby prepared their cakes. What ingredients did Max use? Ruby? Invite students to brainstorm different kinds of cake they might like to make.

3. Provide each child with a box and a copy of the cake mix box patterns (page 57). Students will also need construction paper, tape, glue, scissors, and crayons or markers. Tell students to cover their boxes with construction paper, folding the paper around the corners and securing the edges with tape.

4. Have children complete the fill-in forms, cut them out along the dotted lines, and then glue them to the box. (Point out that the front of the box is a good place for the cake name and picture, while the narrow side of the box works well for the ingredients list.) Stock a shelf with children's completed cake mix boxes, and invite them to visit the display and spend some time daydreaming about delectable desserts.

Uh-Oh Stories (Language Arts)

Use one of the most memorable lines of the story's text ("But it was too late") as a springboard for writing storybooks. To introduce this writing activity, reread the story with students. As a group, discuss the main problem in the story. You may ask a few volunteers to retell what happened when Max tried to join Ruby in the kitchen, and ways Max was able to help Ruby.

1. Explain that students will be writing a new adventure for Max and Ruby—a story in which Max has the same kind of problem— foiling everything Ruby tries to do. Tell children that their new stories will incorporate that same line: "But it was too late." Give each child a copy of the story strips (page 58), four sheets of white paper, and one sheet of construction paper. Students will also need glue sticks, scissors, pencils, and crayons or markers.

Tip

▲▲▲▲▲▲

Model steps two through five to guide students in constructing their books. When students are ready to write (steps six and seven), model on chart paper the structure of the story for them to use as reference.

2. Tell children to fold their sheet of construction paper in half. The folded paper will serve as the book's front and back cover.

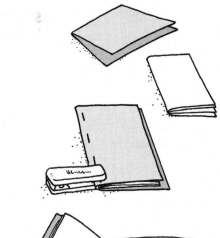

3. To assemble the books, have children place all their sheets of white paper in a stack and then fold the stack in half. Explain that the folded sheets will become the interior of the book, the blank pages where students will write their stories.

4. Have children place the folded white sheets inside the construction paper cover, keeping all the folds together. Tell students to staple the sheets together along the folded edge, forming the book's spine.

5. Before children begin writing (and it's too late!), have them cut out the sentence strips and glue the strips onto every other white page (beginning with the second page).

6. Invite children to write and illustrate their new Max stories. Encourage students to write and illustrate in whichever order they choose.

7. Have students label their book's cover with their name as well as the title of the story. Then have children bring home the book to share and read with families.

Not-Allowed Signs (Language Arts)

Ruby eventually becomes so frustrated with Max's blundering in the kitchen that she bars his entry. She makes a sign that features a picture of Max with a line through it—a sign that meant "Max, the kitchen is no place for you." Though that's what the sign meant to Max, who doesn't yet know how to read, Ruby didn't use words to make her meaning clear. Explore how this same wordless message technique is used around the world as an international way of saying a specific activity or object is prohibited.

1. Take students on a tour of the school, looking for not-allowed signs. For example, you may find that there is a "No parking" sign by the building's front doors and a "No food or drinks" sign on the library door.

2. Give each child an index card to take home. Tell students that they have a homework assignment—to look for not-allowed signs when

(continued)

Pumpkin Soup

by Helen Cooper

(Farrar, Straus and Giroux, 1999)

A cat, squirrel, and duck each contribute to making an extraordinary pumpkin soup.

The Story of Ferdinand

by Munro Leaf

(Viking, 1936)

Unlike the other Spanish bulls his age, Ferdinand enjoys smelling flowers and sitting under his favorite cork tree.

they are out with their families or caregivers. Explain that on the index card, each child will draw a picture of the sign and write in his or her own words what the sign means. Examples of signs children might find include "No crossing," "No smoking," and "No cell phones." Assist children who are unable to search for or locate signs outside of school in completing the assignment (for example, by finding a sign on the school bus or around the school).

3. Post the sign collection in a classroom display and invite students to discuss ways in which "not allowed signs" may be helpful or unhelpful to people in the community.

A Mixing Bowl of Words (Language Arts)

Use the baking-related illustrations printed on the endpapers of *Bunny Cakes* as inspiration for a vocabulary-building word wall—a word wall shaped like a mixing bowl!

1. To make the mixing bowl, cut a large bowl shape from white craft paper. On it, glue a wooden cooking spoon. Once the glue is dry, attach the bowl to a wall or bulletin board.

2. Invite students to turn the mixing bowl into a word wall with words related to baking—for example, *spatula, flour,* and *whisk.* As children brainstorm, write their words on the bowl. Encourage students to refer to the word wall as they write and illustrate their own stories about baking.

Premium Cake Mix

(Write the name of the cake.)

(Draw a picture of the baked, decorated cake.)

Net weight: 18 ounces of fun!

Guaranteed to be delicious by

(Write your name.)

Ingredients
(List what this cake is made of.)

But it was too late.

But it was too late.

But it was too late.

But it was too late.

But it was too late.

But it was too late.

But it was too late.

But it was too late.

But it was too late.

But it was too late.

But it was too late.

But it was too late.

But it was too late.

But it was too late.

Bunny Mail

❖

(PENGUIN, 2004)

Max's letter finds its way to Grandma. Grandma writes back. Soon Grandma learns that while Max enjoys their correspondence, he's really writing to ask for something in particular.

Before Reading

As a group, discuss writing, sending, and reading correspondence such as postcards, invitations, cards, letters, and e-mails. Invite students to share what they know about what happens to a traditional letter once it's mailed—who handles it, where it goes, and how it's transported from place to place.

After Reading

Have students examine the illustrations and talk about the lift-the-flap format of the book. Do children think that the format helps the author tell the story? Why or why not? Use these questions to explore other details of the story:

◎ Why did Grandma end up with Max's letter to Santa? Did Grandma understand what Max had written in his letter? How do you know?

◎ How does Max feel when he receives the bulldozer letter? The airplane letter? What about when the package arrives, postmarked from the North Pole?

Messages and Themes

◆ People write and mail letters to communicate with others.

◆ Mail carriers deliver mail.

May 5, 2008

Dear Grandma,
We read Bunny Mail. How did you know what Max was wishing for? Do you know Santa? We write letters at school when it's Valentine's Day. Maybe we'll send a valentine to you this year.   Sincerely,
Miss Perry's Class

Tip

Along with setting up a class post office center, invite students to make mailboxes for sending and receiving mail. For details, see You've Got Mailboxes! (page 61).

Dear Character (Language Arts)

Use the read-aloud experience as a springboard for writing as a group and learning about letter-writing conventions in particular.

1. Explain that together you'll be writing an informal letter to a character in the story. Invite children to tell what they know about writing letters (format and content).

2. Together, choose a character and challenge students to think specifically about what makes that character special. What questions would they like to ask that character about what happened in the story? Are there bits of classroom news that the character may be interested in learning about? What other topics might interest him or her?

3. On chart paper, record students' collaborative letter. As you write, make the most of this opportunity to talk about letter writing with children. Have them think about how a formal letter may look and what the content may include—from deciding where the date goes to choosing a salutation to close the letter.

4. Wrap up the writing experience by having students write their own letters using the collaborative letter as a model. Finally, display all the letters, alongside a copy of the book, in the classroom library.

A Post Office Center (Social Studies, Language Arts)

Inspire daily writing (and reading) with a classroom post office center.

1. To get started, have students brainstorm what they'll need in the designated area. Record their ideas on chart paper. Suggestions may include dramatic play props you can gather from other centers in the room, such as cash registers, play money, rubber stamps, and a scale. Suggestions may also include consumable goods, such as stamps, envelopes, stationery, and mailing labels.

2. Collect as many of these items as possible, and have students set up the center. If children feel that key components of a real-life post office are missing, invite them to create what they can from readily obtainable materials. For example, if children wish they had mailbags, provide students with brown paper bags they can paint and decorate with postal colors and symbols.

3. Stock the post office center with copies of the reproducible letter pattern and bunny stamps (page 62). Demonstrate for students

how to cut along the dashed cut lines of the letter pattern and fold along the solid lines. Model composing a friendly letter, noting the mailing and return addresses, and attaching the stamp. Seal the letter with tape, a sticker, or a glue stick.

4. Kick off the grand opening of the new center by taking a class field trip to a local post office. Or take a tour of the mailroom at your school, where teachers send and receive mail. When you return to the classroom, invite children to explain what they learned about how a post office works. Then provide students with time to explore and use their brand-new post office amenities.

You've Got Mailboxes! (Language Arts, Math)

Make personalized mailboxes, perfect for receiving mystery mail!

1. In advance, invite families to send in empty shoe boxes. Provide each child with a box to decorate.

2. Have each student use a permanent marker to label the mailbox with only his or her street number. Or assign a random number to each child. (In this way, students' home street addresses remain confidential.) Place the mailboxes in the class post office center.

3. Label envelopes with numbers that correspond to the mailboxes, and place the envelopes in a paper bag. Place the bag at the post office center. As children visit the center, invite them to choose an envelope from the bag and use the letter template and stamps (page 62) to write a letter to a mystery student. (Allow students to dictate their letters as necessary.)

4. Have students place their letter in the matching envelope and deliver it to the matching mailbox. You might allow a week or so for all students to visit the center and write a letter, having children wait until everyone has mail to open the letters. At the end of the week, have children check their mailboxes and read their mystery letters. Can they guess who sent them a letter?

Book Links

Dear Mr. Blueberry
by James Simon
(McElderry Books, 1991)

When Emily wants to learn more about her whale, Arthur, she sends a letter to her teacher Mr. Blueberry. Before long the pair, teacher and student, become correspondents—sharing stories and advice in their letters about an improbable whale.

Tell-a-Bunny
by Nancy Elizabeth Wallace
(Winslow Press, 2000)

A surprise party is transformed into a sunrise party, when telephone messages between bunnies go awry.

Tip

For extra writing and math practice, continue this letter-writing activity for a few weeks. At the start of each day, invite a few children to work together in order to place the mailboxes in numeric order from lowest to highest, highest to lowest, in groups of odds and evens, or another order.

Bunny Mail

Fold here.

Dear _____,

_____

_____

_____

Fold here.

_____

_____

_____ ,

_____

Author Study Celebration

Wrap up reading and exploring favorite Rosemary Wells books by having an author study celebration. Here are some activities you can depend on for learning-filled fun:

A Book-Buddy Bash

Invite students to share their favorite Rosemary Wells books with children in another classroom. For example, your students may host older students who can read with them. To help older children develop reading confidence and prepare for the event, you may encourage them to practice reading aloud independently or with a partner. After the book buddies have read together, consider having students share a special snack inspired by Yoko. Sushi? Franks and beans? Potato knishes, anyone?

Character Riddle

Invite children to practice writing questions and hone critical-thinking skills by writing riddles about favorite Rosemary Wells characters.

1. Have each student recall two details about a character that could be turned into riddle clues. For example, a child writing a riddle about Yoko may recall that Yoko's lunch cooler was made of willow and contained rice rolls.

2. To write the riddle, students weave their details into a question, such as "Which character has a willow cooler and likes to eat rice rolls for lunch?"

3. Provide each child with a sheet of paper to fold in half. Have students write the riddle on the top flap and its answer on the bottom flap. Display the riddles in the classroom (or in the library), and encourage children to read and solve one another's riddles.

▲▲▲▲▲▲▲▲▲▲▲▲▲▲▲▲▲▲▲▲

Additional Books by Rosemary Wells

Eduardo Cumpleanos en la Piscina
(Santillana, 1996)

Eduardo el Primer Dia de Colegio
(Santillana, 1997)

Edward in Deep Water
(Penguin Putnam, 1995)

Edward's Overwhelming Overnight
(Penguin Putnam, 1995)

Edward Unready for School
(Penguin Putnam, 1995)

Felix and the Worrier
(Candlewick, 2003)

Felix Feels Better
(Candlewick, 2001)

Fritz and the Mess Fairy
(Dial, 1991)

Hazel's Amazing Mother
(Dial, 1985)

Here Comes Mother Goose
(Candlewick, 1999)

Morris's Disappearing Bag
(Dial, 1975)

My Very First Mother Goose
(Candlewick, 1996)

Nora la Revoltosa
(Dial, 1997)

The Small World of Binky Braverman
(Viking, 2003)

For a full listing of Rosemary Wells books available on read-along audiotape, audio CD, animated video, DVD, and other nonbook formats, visit Weston Woods at Scholastic Inc. (www.teacher .scholastic.com/products/westonwoods/ index.htm).

▼▼▼▼▼▼▼▼▼▼▼▼▼▼▼▼▼▼▼▼

And the Secret Survey Says . . .

Place the Rosemary Wells books you've read along a whiteboard ledge, and have children choose four as class favorites. Explain that students will work in small groups to make a poster for each book selected. Provide each group with oak tag, construction paper, markers, and other art materials. Display the completed posters and take a secret-ballot vote for the class's favorite book. Then share the story that gathered the most votes as a read aloud. Be sure to leave up all the posters during the class's author study festivities. Then consider loaning them to the library to encourage other young readers.

Unforgettable Classroom Guests

Borrow bigger-than-life costumes for the characters Timothy and Ruby! The costumes are available through Costume Specialists of Penguin Putnam Books for Young Readers. Arrange to borrow the costumes several months in advance of the celebration. Plan to cover related shipping costs. For more information, call (800) 596-9357. Or visit penguinputnam.com/static/ packages/us/yreaders-new/costumes-start.html.